Instant Zest Rice & Grain Cookbook for Beginners

Easy, Delicious & Healthy Recipes for Smart People on a Budget (21-Day Meal Plan)

Megan Jamsen

© Copyright 2020 Megan Jamsen - All Rights Reserved.

In no way is it legal to reproduce, duplicate, or transmit any part of this document by either electronic means or in printed format. Recording of this publication is strictly prohibited, and any storage of this material is not allowed unless with written permission from the publisher. All rights reserved.

The information provided herein is stated to be truthful and consistent, in that any liability, regarding inattention or otherwise, by any usage or abuse of any policies, processes, or directions contained within is the solitary and complete responsibility of the recipient reader. Under no circumstances will any legal liability or blame be held against the publisher for any reparation, damages, or monetary loss due to the information herein, either directly or indirectly.

Respective authors own all copyrights not held by the publisher.

Legal Notice:

This book is copyright protected. This is only for personal use. You cannot amend, distribute, sell, use, quote or paraphrase any part of the content within this book without the consent of the author or copyright owner. Legal action will be pursued if this is breached.

Disclaimer Notice:

Please note the information contained within this document is for educational and entertainment purposes only. Every attempt has been made to provide accurate, up-to-date and reliable, complete information. No warranties of any kind are expressed or implied. Readers acknowledge that the author is not engaging in the rendering of legal, financial, medical or professional advice.

By reading this document, the reader agrees that under no circumstances are we responsible for any losses, direct or indirect, which are incurred as a result of the use of information contained within this document, including, but not limited to, errors, omissions, or inaccuracies.

Table of contents

Chapter 1: Understanding the Instant Zest Rice and Grain Cooker 6
- Why Select the Instant Zest Rice and Grain Cooker? 6
- How to Initialize the Instant Zest Rice and Grain Cooker? 7
- What are the Features of the Instant Zest Rice and Grain Cooker? 8
- Variants of the Instant Zest Rice and Grain Cooker 8
- Getting Started with the Instant Zest Rice and Grain Cooker 9
- Precautions 9
- Understanding the Smart Programs 10
- FAQs 11

Chapter 2: 21 Days Meal Plan 12
- Week 01 12
- Week 02 13
- Week 03 15

Chapter 3: White Rice Recipes 17
- Simple White Rice 17
- Paella Rice 18
- Egg Fried Rice 20
- Baja Chicken Rice 22
- Cajun Rice 24
- Broccoli Pesto Chicken and Rice 26
- Chicken and Rice with Mint Pesto 28
- Spanish Rice 30
- Multigrain Pilaf 31
- Multigrain Cereal Rice 32
- Italian Basmati Rice 33
- Chicken Rice Congee 34
- Chinese Sticky Rice 36
- Chicken Alfredo Rice Casserole 37
- Pecan White Rice 38
- Creamy Garlic Chicken and Rice 39

Chapter 4: Brown Rice Recipes 40
- Simple Brown Rice 40
- Chicken Burrito Bowls 41
- Lentil and Brown Rice Tacos 42

Balsamic Brown Rice Bowl 43
Black Beans with Brown Rice 44
Tomato, Brown Rice and Chickpea Stew 45
Spiced Lentils with Brown Rice and Chicken 46
Brown Rice Pilaf 48
Chicken and Wild Brown Rice 49
Wild Brown Rice with Cranberries 50
Cumin and Parsley Brown Rice 51
Chicken Tikka Masala Brown Rice 52
Caramelized Ginger Chicken with Sticky Rice 54
Thai Sweet Brown Rice with Mango 56
Chicken Veggies and Rice 57
Garlic Butter Chicken and Rice 58

Chapter 5: Lentils 60
Red Lentil Curry 60
Lentil Stew with Mustard Greens 61
Barley and Lentil Salad with Goat Cheese 62
Lentil with Cabbage Slaw 63
Winter Lentil Soup 65
Curried Lentils with Chicken and Potatoes 66
Lentil Stew with Oranges 67
Balsamic-Glazed Pork with Lentils 69
Salmon with Warm Lentil Salad 71
Red lentils with cauliflower and peanuts 73
Halibut with Lentils and Mustard Sauce 75

Chapter 6: Beans 77
Big Beans and Tomato Vinaigrette 77
Green Bean Casserole 79
Garlic Green Beans with Parmesan 81
Party time Beans 82
Black-Eyed Peas with Ham 83
Vibrant Black-Eyed Pea Salad 84
Perfect Pinto Beans 85
Green Beans and Bacon 86
Escarole with Cannellini Beans 87
Marinated Beans with Celery and Ricotta Salata 89

Chapter 7: Steamed Vegetables 90
    Steamed Potatoes 90
    Steamed Pumpkin 91
    Steamed Vegetables with Chile-Lime Butter 92
    Steamed Vegetables with Sesame-Chile Oil 93
    Steamed Baby Vegetables 94
    Steamed Brussels Sprouts and Bacon 95
    Steamed Vegetables with Herb Stir-Ins 97
    Ginger Garlic Steamed Vegetables 98
    Steamed Carrots with Butter 100
    Steamed Carrots 101
    Steamed Carrots with Garlic-Ginger Butter 102
    Steamed Cauliflower with Herbs 103
Conclusion 104

Chapter 1: Understanding the Instant Zest Rice and Grain Cooker

The Instant Zest Rice and Grain Cooker have been manufactured by the makers of the Instant Pot. It is available in the market with three different variants depending upon their sizes. The Instant Zest Rice and Grain Cooker have taken the cooking world with a storm by providing the ultimate sense of easiness, convenience, and value to the users across the globe.

It has been programmed with various 'Smart Programs' for cooking purposes to ensure that your meals are served to you as per your required taste, color, and of course, without having any compromise on retaining the natural taste of the nutrients. You can preset the cooking times and temperatures for oatmeal, quinoa, brown rice, and white rice, in addition to farro, freekeh, and millet. You can also go for preparing your favorite rice pudding, barley, polenta, and much more with this amazing appliance. You can even go for prepping hearty grains like wheat berries and spelt in a shorter time with the Instant Zest Rice and Grain Cooker that takes a long time in cooking using regular cooking techniques.

Additionally, apart from just cooking rice, you can go for steaming your favorite vegetables, tamales, wontons, fish, cabbages, dumplings, and much more with this amazing appliance. There is a state of the art display and various indicators that keep you informed regarding the status of your meal in the pot while cooking. Functions like Keep Warm and Delay Start are very beneficial in keeping your food warm and ready to serve for you when you are ready for it. In simple words, cooking is just limited to a press of a button, giving you the utmost convenience possible.

Why Select the Instant Zest Rice and Grain Cooker?

There are various reasons to choose the Instant Zest Rice and Grain Cooker for your kitchen and change your entire approach towards food. Some of these are explained as follows:

1. The Perfect Way to Cook Grains and Rice

The Instant Zest Rice and Grain Cooker are not just made for cooking rises; it goes beyond the horizons of the world of rice to grains. You can prepare quinoa, oatmeal, and much more with this amazing alliance with merely pressing a few buttons.

2. Cooking with a Single Button

The Instant Zest Rice and Grain Cooker have been developed with the Smart programs for cooking, which are your gateway to ensuring the perfect cooking time and temperatures for preparing your foods like oatmeal, brown rice, white rice, and much more with just a single button.

3. The Smartest Appliance

You don't have to worry about calculating weights, cooking times, and temperatures while using Instant Zest Rice and Grain Cooker. Just select the Smart program, and you are good to go.

4. State of the Art Quality

The inner lid of the Instant Zest Rice and Grain Cooker is made with stainless steel. Moreover, the inner pot is made with aluminum and lined with a non-stick ceramic, which makes it very easy and convenient to clean. It is rust-free and is designed to last for long.

5. Trustworthiness

The success and reliance of Instant Pot have been a prevailing fact in recent times, with so many positive reviews across the world. The Instant Zest Rice and Grain Cooker are manufactured by the same team, keeping the requirements of the modern-day world and ensuring that you get the perfect tasty meals with retaining the natural taste and color of the ingredients.

How to Initialize the Instant Zest Rice and Grain Cooker?

Initializing the Instant Zest Rice and Grain Cooker is not that hard and just requires a few easy steps to change your approach towards cooking. These steps involve the following:

- Remove the packaging, both from inside and outside, and ensure that your appliance is in perfect condition.
- Put the cooker on a level surface and away from any external heat source.
- Go thoroughly through the Safety, Maintenance, and Warranty manual to understand your product more befittingly and avoid any mishap to both the product and yourself.
- Properly wash and clean the device according to the instructions provided in the Safety, Maintenance, and Warranty manual.
- Don't peel off any warning stickers or the rating table from the device.

What are the Features of the Instant Zest Rice and Grain Cooker?

The Instant Zest Rice and Grain Cooker come with many states of the art specs which makes it very convenient and according to modern needs. These include:

- Lightweight, compact, easy in usage.
- Bright, easily read LED display which shows cooking time and cooking options.
- Adjustable cooking time concerning the added ingredients with the smart design program.
- Precise cooking temperature for perfectly cooked rice and grains.
- Steam your vegetables or fish in the steamer tray while cooking your rice at the same time.
- Non-stick, large inner pot, and all other accessories are dishwasher safe.
- Keep Warm, Steam, and Delay Start Functions.
- In-built protection from overheating.

Variants of the Instant Zest Rice and Grain Cooker

There are mainly three different variants of the Instant Zest Rice and Grain Cooker depending upon their sizes. The prices are slightly raised with the rise in the size of the appliance. These include the following:

- Instant Pot Zest 8 Cup
- Instant Pot Zest 20 Cup
- Instant Pot Zest Plus 20 Cup

Getting Started with the Instant Zest Rice and Grain Cooker

The following steps will make you familiar with how to start using your Instant Zest Rice and Grain Cooker.

- Press the lid release button placed on the downside of the lid handle for opening the lid.
- Take out the inner pot from the base of the cooker.
- Add your ingredients to the pot as per your recipe.
- Put back the inner pot on the cooker base.
- Afterward, close the lid. A ticking sound will indicate the proper closing of the lid.
- Power in the appliance. The display will be showing 'OFF,' meaning the device is on standby.
- Chose a Smart Program of your choice.
- Use + / - for manual adjustment of cooking time, if applicable.
- Use 'Start' for starting the cooking procedure; the display will show 'ON.' Manual cooking functions will display a countdown timer on display.
- After the accomplishment of the Smart Program, the device will display 'END' and get into the 'Keep Warm' mode. You can cancel this function by merely pressing the 'Cancel' button.
- When you are ready, press the lid release button and open the lid carefully.

Precautions

The following precautions are important for the safety of the device and yourself before using the device. These include:

- Don't use the device on a stovetop.
- Don't place the device near to any external heat source as it will damage the device.
- You can be exposed to hazardous chemicals like Bisphenol and Lead with this product. They can cause health hazards, so keep yourself safe.

Understanding the Smart Programs

For understanding the cooking times, the following table is just a recommendation. You should follow the required recipe instructions to have a much better and perfect end result.

Smart Program	Estimated Cooking Time	Grain : Water Ratio	Notes
White Rice	25 to 60 minutes	1 cup : 1 ½ cups	The cooking time is adjusted by the cooker automatically after assessing the volume of the grain.
Barley	40 to 90 minutes	1 cup : 2 cups	
Brown Rice	40 to 90 minutes	1 cup : 2 cups	
Couscous	15 to 40 minutes	1 cup : 1 cup	
Mixed Grains	40 to 90 minutes	1 cup : 2 cups	
Bulgur / Cracked Wheat	30 to 60 minutes	1 cup : 1 ½ cups	
Quinoa	30 to 60 minutes	1 cup : 1 ½ cups	
Oatmeal	20 to 90 minutes	1 cup : 3 cups	It will manually set the cooking time.

It is important to understand that all the below explained Smart Functions have adjustable cooking times.

Smart Program	Estimated Cook Time	Temperature	Notes
Steam	5 to 60 minutes	100°C / 212°F	Using a steamer basket and keeping your food off of the boiling hot water will be very beneficial in reserving the minerals and vitamins.
Slow Cook	30 minutes to 24 hours	Low / High	Use the 'Slow Cook' button prior to pressing 'Start' to alter between 'High' and 'Low.' This is compatible with all recipes made with the slow cooker.

Sauté	1 to 30 minutes	Low / High	Never shut the lid while using Sauté. Use the 'Sauté button prior to pressing 'Start' to alter between 'High' and 'Low.'
Manual Keep Warm	up to 12 hours	Low / High	Use the 'Slow Cook' button prior to pressing 'Start' to alter between 'High' and 'Low.' This is compatible with all recipes made with the slow cooker.
Risotto	30 to 60 minutes	Auto	Sauté desired veggies and dry rice prior to adding liquid.

FAQs

1. Why do we need the Instant Zest Rice and Grain Cooker?

Rice cookers are very convenient in saving time and prepping delicious and nutritious meals. They can be used for making both grains and rice for side dishes and main dishes. You can also make oatmeal, cook meat, steam veggies, and make single-pot dishes in a go.

2. What kind of rice can the Instant Zest Rice and Grain Cooker prepare?

It is designed with a preset Smart Program for various known types of rice and grains. You can also make sorghum, spelt, wild rice, brown rice, oats, quinoa, bulgur, white rice, lentils, corn, barley, farro, and much more with it.

Chapter 2: 21 Days Meal Plan

Week 01

Day 1

Breakfast: Big Beans and Tomato Vinaigrette

Lunch: Barley and Lentil Salad with Goat Cheese

Snack: Steamed Potatoes

Dinner: Chicken Burrito Bowls

Day 2

Breakfast: Green Bean Casserole

Lunch: Lentil Fritter Pitas with Red Cabbage Slaw

Snack: Steamed Pumpkin

Dinner: Lentil and Brown Rice Tacos

Day 3

Breakfast: Garlic Green Beans with Parmesan

Lunch: Halibut with Lentils and Mustard Sauce

Snack: Steamed Vegetables with Chile-Lime Butter

Dinner: Balsamic Brown Rice Bowl

Day 4

Breakfast: Party time Beans

Lunch: Curried red lentils with fried cauliflower and peanuts

Snack: Steamed Asparagus Medley

Dinner: Black Beans with Brown Rice

Day 5

Breakfast: Black-Eyed Peas with Ham

Lunch: Warm lentil and baby carrot salad with labneh

Snack: Steamed Baby Vegetables

Dinner: Tomato, Brown Rice and Chickpea Stew

Day 6

Breakfast: Vibrant Black-Eyed Pea Salad

Lunch: Salmon with Warm Lentil Salad

Snack: Steamed Brussels Sprouts and Bacon

Dinner: Spiced Lentils with Brown Rice and Chicken

Day 7

Breakfast: Perfect Pinto Beans

Lunch: Balsamic-Glazed Pork with Lentils

Snack: Steamed Vegetables with Herb Stir-Ins

Dinner: Brown Rice Pilaf

Week 02

Day 1

Breakfast: Green Beans and Bacon

Lunch: Lentil Stew with Oranges

Snack: Steamed Carrots with Butter

Dinner: Chicken and Wild Brown Rice

Day 2

Breakfast: Escarole with Cannellini Beans

Lunch: Curried Lentils with Chicken and Potatoes

Snack: Steamed Carrots

Dinner: Wild Brown Rice with Cranberries

Day 3

Breakfast: Marinated Beans with Celery and Ricotta Salata

Lunch: Winter Lentil Soup

Snack: Steamed Carrots with Garlic-Ginger Butter

Dinner: Cumin and Parsley Brown Rice

Day 4

Breakfast: Big Beans and Tomato Vinaigrette

Lunch: Lentil with Cabbage Slaw

Snack: Steamed Cauliflower with Herbs

Dinner: Chicken Tikka Masala Brown Rice

Day 5

Breakfast: Green Bean Casserole

Lunch: Barley and Lentil Salad with Goat Cheese

Snack: Steamed Potatoes

Dinner: Caramelized Ginger Chicken with Sticky Rice

Day 6

Breakfast: Garlic Green Beans with Parmesan

Lunch: Lentil Stew with Mustard Greens

Snack: Steamed Pumpkin

Dinner: Thai Sweet Brown Rice with Mango

Day 7

Breakfast: Party time Beans

Lunch: Red Lentil Curry

Snack: Steamed Vegetables with Chile-Lime Butter

Dinner: Chicken Veggies and Rice

Week 03

Day 1

Breakfast: Big Beans and Tomato Vinaigrette

Lunch: Barley and Lentil Salad with Goat Cheese

Snack: Steamed Potatoes

Dinner: Chicken Burrito Bowls

Day 2

Breakfast: Green Bean Casserole

Lunch: Lentil with Cabbage Slaw

Snack: Steamed Pumpkin

Dinner: Lentil and Brown Rice Tacos

Day 3

Breakfast: Garlic Green Beans with Parmesan

Lunch: Halibut with Lentils and Mustard Sauce

Snack: Steamed Vegetables with Chile-Lime Butter

Dinner: Balsamic Brown Rice Bowl

Day 4

Breakfast: Party time Beans

Lunch: Red lentils with fried cauliflower and peanuts

Snack: Steamed Asparagus Medley

Dinner: Black Beans with Brown Rice

Day 5

Breakfast: Black-Eyed Peas with Ham

Lunch: Warm lentil and baby carrot salad with labneh

Snack: Steamed Baby Vegetables

Dinner: Tomato, Brown Rice and Chickpea Stew

Day 6

Breakfast: Vibrant Black-Eyed Pea Salad

Lunch: Salmon with Warm Lentil Salad

Snack: Steamed Brussels Sprouts and Bacon

Dinner: Spiced Lentils with Brown Rice and Chicken

Day 7

Breakfast: Perfect Pinto Beans

Lunch: Balsamic-Glazed Pork with Lentils

Snack: Steamed Vegetables with Herb Stir-Ins

Dinner: Brown Rice Pilaf

Chapter 3: White Rice Recipes

Simple White Rice

Total Time: 30 minutes
Servings: 4

Ingredients:

- 1 cup white rice
- 1¼ cups water
- 1 pinch salt

Method:

1. Put rice, water, and salt in the Instant Zest Rice and Grain Cooker.
2. Secure the lid and press the "White Rice" button.
3. Instant Zest Cooker will automatically shut down when the rice is completely cooked.
4. Fluff the rice and dish out to serve hot.

Nutritional Value:

- Calories 169
- Total Fat 0.3 g
- Saturated Fat 0.1 g
- Cholesterol 0 mg
- Sodium 467 mg
- Total Carbs 37 g
- Sugar 0.1 g
- Fiber 0.6 g
- Protein 3.3 g

Paella Rice

Total Time: 40 minutes
Servings: 4

Ingredients:

- ½ cup white rice
- 7 oz diced tomatoes
- 2 cloves garlic, minced
- ½ teaspoon cayenne pepper
- 1 tablespoon dry white wine
- ½ cup frozen peas
- Lemon wedges, for serving
- ½ pound boneless skinless chicken breasts, cut into 1" pieces
- Kosher salt and black pepper, to taste
- ½ large onion, chopped
- 1 teaspoon paprika
- 1 cup low-sodium chicken broth
- ½ pound medium shrimp, peeled and deveined
- ½ teaspoon extra-virgin olive oil
- ¼ pound chorizo, sliced
- 2 tablespoons heavy cream

Method:

1. Put oil in the Instant Zest Rice and Grain Cooker and add chicken, chorizo, salt, and black pepper.
2. Press "Sauté" and adjust the timer to 10 minutes.
3. Stir in the rice along with the rest of the ingredients.
4. Secure the lid and press the "White Rice" button.
5. Open the lid and add shrimps and frozen peas.
6. Press "Steam" and set the timer for about 20 minutes.
7. Dish out the paella rice and serve warm.

Nutritional Value:

- Calories 450
- Total Fat 19.5 g
- Saturated Fat 7.1 g
- Cholesterol 197 mg
- Sodium 567 mg
- Total Carbs 27.2 g
- Sugar 3.2 g
- Fiber 2.7 g
- Protein 39.6 g

Egg Fried Rice

Total Time: 45 minutes
Servings: 8

Ingredients:

- 2 teaspoons black pepper
- 4 teaspoons Worcestershire sauce
- 4 eggs, whisked
- 6 cups of water
- 4 tablespoons salted butter
- 4 teaspoons low-sodium soy sauce
- 1 cup frozen peas
- 1 cup frozen edamame
- 4 cups dry white rice
- 1 cup frozen carrots, diced
- 1 cup frozen roasted corn
- 2 teaspoons shallot, minced

Method:

1. Put butter in the Instant Zest Rice and Grain Cooker and stir in the whisked eggs.
2. Press "Sauté" and adjust the timer to 2 minutes.
3. Open the lid and add the rest of the ingredients.
4. Secure the lid and press the "White Rice" button.
5. Instant Zest Cooker will automatically shut down when the rice is completely cooked.
6. Fluff the rice and dish out to serve hot.

Nutritional Value:

- Calories 504
- Total Fat 10.3 g
- Saturated Fat 4.7 g
- Cholesterol 97 mg
- Sodium 281 mg
- Total Carbs 86.7 g
- Sugar 4.6 g
- Fiber 5.3 g

- Protein 14.8 g

Baja Chicken Rice

Total Time: 1 hour
Servings: 12

Ingredients:

Chicken Rice:

- 2 tablespoons fresh lime juice
- ½ cup black beans
- 1/3 cup fresh orange juice
- ¼ cup extra-virgin olive oil, divided
- Salt and black pepper, to taste
- ½ teaspoon ground cumin
- 2 cups white rice
- 3 cups of water
- ½ teaspoon oregano
- ½ teaspoon garlic powder
- 1-pound chicken breasts, diced
- ½ teaspoon paprika

For The Mango Salsa

- 1½ cups mango, chopped
- 3 tablespoons lime juice
- ½ small red onion, finely chopped
- 1 clove garlic, minced
- 1 tablespoon fresh cilantro, chopped

Method:

1. Mix together 2 tablespoons of olive oil, lime juice, orange juice, oregano, cumin, garlic powder, and paprika in a large bowl.
2. Coat the chicken breasts in the marinade.
3. Cover the bowl with plastic wrap and refrigerate for about 2 hours.
4. Meanwhile, mix together mango, salt, red onion, garlic, cilantro, and lime juice in a medium bowl and refrigerate.

5. Put the remaining olive oil in the Instant Zest Rice and Grain Cooker and add the marinated chicken.
6. Press "Sauté" and adjust the timer to 5 minutes.
7. Open the lid and add rice and water.
8. Secure the lid and press the "White Rice" button.
9. Instant Zest Cooker will automatically shut down when the rice is completely cooked.
10. Add chicken and mango salsa to the Instant Zest Cooker and press "Steam."
11. Steam for about 10 minutes and dish out in a bowl to serve.

Nutritional Value:

- Calories 268
- Total Fat 7.4 g
- Saturated Fat 1.5 g
- Cholesterol 34 mg
- Sodium 281 mg
- Total Carbs 34.7 g
- Sugar 3.9 g
- Fiber 2.2 g
- Sodium 37 mg
- Protein 15.3 g

Cajun Rice

Total Time: 50 minutes
Servings: 10

Ingredients:

- 4 andouille sausages, cut into 1-inch pieces
- 4 large chicken breasts, cut into 1-inch pieces
- Kosher salt and black pepper, to taste
- 4 cups chicken stock
- 2 teaspoons Cajun seasoning
- 6 green onions, sliced
- 2 cups white rice
- 2 medium onions, chopped
- 1 red bell pepper, chopped
- 4 garlic cloves, minced
- 30 oz tomato sauce
- 2 cups cheddar cheese
- 2 tablespoons olive oil
- 1 green bell pepper, chopped

Method:

1. Season the chicken breast with Cajun seasoning, salt, and black pepper.
2. Put olive oil in the Instant Zest Rice and Grain Cooker and add chicken breasts and sausages.
3. Press "Sauté" and sauté for about 5 minutes until browned.
4. Stir in the garlic and tomato sauce and sauté for about 1 more minute.
5. Stir in the rice and remaining ingredients and secure the lid.
6. Press "White Rice" button and allow it to cook.
7. Instant Zest Cooker will automatically shut down when the rice is completely cooked.
8. Dish out in a bowl and serve warm.

Nutritional Value:

- Calories 521
- Total Fat 24.4 g
- Saturated Fat 9.7 g
- Cholesterol 95 mg
- Sodium 1357 mg
- Total Carbs 41.1 g
- Sugar 6.7 g
- Fiber 2.8 g
- Protein 33.6 g

Broccoli Pesto Chicken and Rice

Total Time: 50 minutes
Servings: 10

Ingredients:

- 2 cups jasmine rice
- 2 cups fresh basil
- ½ cup Parmesan cheese, freshly grated
- 2 garlic cloves
- 1½ cups water
- 16 bone-in, skin-on chicken thighs
- Crushed red pepper flakes, for garnish
- 4 small heads broccoli, florets removed and blanched, divided
- 1 cup extra-virgin olive oil, divided
- ½ cup of raw almonds
- 2 teaspoons kosher salt
- 2 teaspoons black pepper

Method:

1. Put rice and water in the Instant Zest Rice and Grain Cooker.
2. Secure the lid and press the "White Rice" button.
3. Instant Zest Cooker will automatically shut down when the rice is completely cooked.
4. Meanwhile, put the broccoli, Parmesan, basil, almonds, salt, garlic, and ½ cup of oil in a food processor and blend until combined.
5. Heat oil in a large skillet and add chicken thighs, salt, and black pepper.
6. Cook for about 5 minutes on each side and transfer into the Instant Zest Cooker along with the broccoli and pesto.
7. Press "Steam" and set the timer for about 8 minutes.
8. Dish out the rice and serve with the sprinkling of red pepper flakes.

Nutritional Value:

- Calories 735
- Total Fat 53.9 g

- Saturated Fat 14.7 g
- Cholesterol 161 mg
- Sodium 678 mg
- Total Carbs 31.8 g
- Sugar 0.6 g
- Fiber 3.2 g
- Protein 32.7 g

Chicken and Rice with Mint Pesto

Total Time: 40 minutes
Servings: 8

Ingredients:

- 1 cup Parmigiano-Reggiano cheese, freshly grated
- ½ cup fresh lemon juice
- 3 cups roast chicken, shredded
- 6 scallions
- 2 cloves garlic
- 2 small cucumbers
- Sea salt, to taste
- 2 cups long-grain white rice
- 4 cups packed fresh mint leaves
- ½ cup pine nuts
- 8 tablespoons extra-virgin olive oil
- 3 cups frozen peas
- 2 cups fresh basil leaves

Method:

1. Mix together mint, basil, ½ cup peas, cucumber, cheese, lemon juice, pine nuts, garlic, 3 tablespoons oil, and ½ teaspoon salt in a food processor.
2. Process until smooth and keep aside.
3. Heat oil in a large skillet and add roast chicken.
4. Cook for about 10 minutes and transfer into the Instant Zest Rice and Grain Cooker along with rice and 1½ cups water.
5. Press "White Rice" and secure the lid.
6. Instant Zest Cooker will automatically shut down when the rice is completely cooked.
7. Stir in mint pesto, mixing thoroughly and dish out to serve.

Nutritional Value:

- Calories 490
- Total Fat 24.1 g

- Saturated Fat 5.1 g
- Cholesterol 10 mg
- Sodium 358 mg
- Total Carbs 50.2 g
- Sugar 4.5 g
- Fiber 5.1 g
- Protein 20.9 g

Spanish Rice

Total Time: 45 minutes
Servings: 8

Ingredients:

- 1 (14.5-ounce) can diced tomatoes
- 2 tablespoons olive oil
- 2 cups low-sodium vegetable broth
- 1½ teaspoons ground cumin
- 1½ teaspoons kosher salt
- 2 cups white rice
- ½ red bell pepper, medium diced
- 2 teaspoons chili powder
- 1 medium yellow onion, chopped
- 1½ cups water
- 3 garlic cloves, minced
- ½ yellow bell pepper, medium diced
- 2 tablespoons fresh cilantro leaves, for garnishing

Method:

1. Put olive oil in the Instant Zest Rice and Grain Cooker and add rice and onions.
2. Press "Sauté" and sauté for about 4 minutes until the rice turns a pale golden brown, stirring continuously.
3. Open the lid and add the rest of the ingredients except cilantro.
4. Secure the lid and press "White Rice."
5. Instant Zest Cooker will automatically shut down when the rice is completely cooked.
6. Garnish with cilantro and serve hot.

Nutritional Value:

- Calories 227
- Total Fat 4.2g
- Saturated Fat 0.6g
- Cholesterol 0mg
- Sodium 469mg
- Total Carbs 42.6g
- Fiber 2g
- Sugars 2.8g
- Protein 4.8g

Multigrain Pilaf

Total Time: 45 minutes

Servings: 6

Ingredients:

- ½ medium onion, finely chopped
- ½ teaspoon dried sage, crushed
- ¼ teaspoon salt
- 2 garlic cloves, minced
- ½ medium red sweet pepper, chopped
- ½ tablespoon butter
- 1/8 teaspoon black pepper
- ¼ cup regular barley, rinsed and drained
- 7-ounce cans vegetable broth or chicken broth
- ½ cup wheat berries, rinsed and drained
- ¼ cup white rice, rinsed and drained
- 1 cup loose-pack frozen baby lima beans

Method:

1. Mix together wheat berries, garlic, barley, broth, soybeans, sweet pepper, onion, butter, sage, salt, black pepper, and rice in the Instant Zest Rice and Grain Cooker.
2. Secure the lid and press the "White Rice" button.
3. Instant Zest Cooker will automatically shut down when the rice is completely cooked.
4. Fluff the rice and dish out to serve hot.

Nutritional Value:

- Calories 132
- Total Fat 1.5g
- Saturated Fat 0.7g
- Cholesterol 3mg
- Sodium 292mg
- Total Carbs 24.4g
- Fiber 3.6g
- Sugars 1.7g
- Protein 5.1g

Multigrain Cereal Rice

Total Time: 40 minutes

Servings: 6

Ingredients:

- 5 cups of water
- 1 teaspoon cinnamon
- 1 teaspoon vanilla extract
- 1 apple, peeled, cored and diced
- ½ cup quinoa, rinsed and drained
- ½ cup steel cut oats
- ½ cup brown rice, rinsed and drained
- ½ cup of wheat berries
- Maple syrup, for serving

Method:

1. Put all the ingredients in the Instant Zest Rice and Grain Cooker.
2. Secure the lid and press the "White Rice" button.
3. Instant Zest Cooker will automatically shut down when the rice is completely cooked.
4. Fluff the multigrain cereal and dish out to serve hot.

Nutritional Value:

- Calories 324
- Total Fat 1.9g
- Saturated Fat 0.3g
- Cholesterol 0mg
- Sodium 4mg
- Total Carbs 39.6g
- Fiber 3.4g
- Sugars 8g
- Protein 4.9g

Italian Basmati Rice

Total Time: 40 minutes

Servings: 4

Ingredients:

- 1 teaspoon Italian seasoning
- 6 green onions, sliced
- 14½ ounces diced tomatoes, drained
- 2 garlic cloves, minced
- 2 cups chicken broth
- 1 cup basmati rice

Method:

1. Put the tomatoes and green onions into the Instant Zest Rice and Grain Cooker.
2. Add the rest of the ingredients and mix well.
3. Secure the lid and press the "White Rice" button.
4. Instant Zest Cooker will automatically shut down when the rice is completely cooked.
5. Fluff the rice and dish out to serve hot.

Nutritional Value:

- Calories 257
- Total Fat 1.6g
- Saturated Fat 0.4g
- Cholesterol 1mg
- Sodium 393mg
- Total Carbs 43.7g
- Fiber 2.5g
- Sugars 3.8g
- Protein 7.1g

Chicken Rice Congee

Total Time: 1 hour
Servings: 12

Ingredients:

- 3 cups jasmine rice
- 8 cups of water
- 12 scallions, 4 whole and 8 thinly sliced
- 4 Chinese sausages
- Chopped roasted peanuts, soy sauce, toasted sesame oil, and hot sauce, for serving
- 16 cups chicken stock
- 8 quarter-size fresh ginger slices, plus ¼ cup fresh ginger, minced
- 4 skinless, boneless chicken breast halves, cut into 1-inch pieces
- Salt, to taste

Method:

1. Mix together the rice, water, stock, ginger, and 2 whole scallions in the Instant Zest Rice and Grain Cooker.
2. Secure the lid and press the "White Rice" button.
3. Instant Zest Cooker will automatically shut down when the rice is completely cooked.
4. Discard the ginger and whole scallions.
5. Meanwhile, cover the Chinese sausages with water in a small saucepan and bring to a boil.
6. Simmer for about 6 minutes and drain the sausages.
7. Add sausages along with the remaining ingredients to the congee and secure the lid.
8. Press the "Steam" button and set the timer for about 15 minutes.
9. Season the congee with salt and ladle out into bowls to serve hot.

Nutritional Value:

- Calories 247
- Total Fat 3.5g

- Saturated Fat 1.1g
- Cholesterol 25mg
- Sodium 1072mg
- Total Carbs 39.8g
- Fiber 2.7g
- Sugars 1.4g
- Protein 13.6g

Chinese Sticky Rice

Total Time: 40 minutes
Servings: 20

Ingredients:

- 6 tablespoons Asian oyster sauce
- 1 cup scallions, thinly sliced (greens only)
- 8 tablespoons regular soy sauce
- 4 cups chicken broth
- 1 teaspoon white pepper
- 8 teaspoons Asian pure sesame oil
- 2 tablespoons fresh ginger, peeled and finely minced
- 2 tablespoons vegetable oil
- 2 cups dried shiitake mushrooms, soaked in water for 1 hour, drained and chopped
- 6 cups uncooked sticky rice, soaked in water for 3-4 hours
- 10 links Chinese Sausage, diced
- 1 cup Chinese cooking rice wine

Method:

1. Put brown rice with all other ingredients in the Instant Zest Rice and Grain Cooker.
2. Secure the lid and press the "White Rice" button.
3. Instant Zest Cooker will automatically shut down when the rice is completely cooked.
4. Fluff the rice and dish out to serve hot.

Nutritional Value:

- Calories 144
- Total Fat 6g
- Saturated Fat 1.4g
- Cholesterol 5mg
- Sodium 822mg
- Total Carbs 18g
- Fiber 1.5g
- Sugars 1.6g
- Protein 4.2g

Chicken Alfredo Rice Casserole

Total Time: 50 minutes
Servings: 12

Ingredients:

- 4 chicken breasts, sliced
- 4 ounces cream cheese
- 1 teaspoon salt
- 4 tablespoons Parmesan cheese
- 1½ cups chicken broth
- 2 head broccoli, chopped
- 3 cups jasmine rice
- 4 tablespoons butter
- ½ teaspoon black pepper
- 5 cups cream
- 8 garlic cloves, minced

Method:

1. Put rice, chicken, garlic, butter, cream cheese, parmesan, cream, broth, salt, and black pepper in the Instant Zest Rice and Grain Cooker.
2. Secure the lid and press the "White Rice" button.
3. Instant Zest Cooker will automatically shut down when the rice is completely cooked.
4. Add the broccoli and secure the lid.
5. Press the "Steam" button and set the timer for about 10 minutes.
6. Fluff the rice and dish out to serve hot.

Nutritional Value:

- Calories 404
- Total Fat 17g   2
- Saturated Fat 9.3g
- Cholesterol 85mg
- Sodium 446mg   1
- Total Carbs 41.3g
- Fiber 2.5g
- Sugars 2.4g
- Protein 20.6g

Pecan White Rice

Total Time: 55 minutes
Servings: 4

Ingredients:

- 12 ounces white rice
- ½ cup carrots, coarsely chopped
- 21 ounces vegetable broth
- 8 ounces button mushrooms, sliced
- 1 tablespoon dairy-free butter
- 3 tablespoons tamari sauce
- ½ teaspoon dried marjoram
- 1 teaspoon of sea salt
- ¼ cup pecans, chopped
- 1/3 cup white onion, diced
- ½ teaspoon dried tarragon
- 1/8 teaspoon black pepper

Method:

1. Put rice blend, broth, carrot, mushrooms, tarragon, butter, marjoram, tamari, onion, salt, and black pepper in the Instant Zest Rice and Grain Cooker.
2. Secure the lid and press the "White Rice" button.
3. Instant Zest Cooker will automatically shut down when the rice is completely cooked.
4. Open the lid and stir in the pecans.
5. Press the "Steam" button and set the timer for about 15 minutes.
6. Instant Zest Cooker will automatically shut down when the rice is completely cooked.
7. Fluff the rice and dish out to serve hot.

Nutritional Value:

- Calories 394
- Total Fat 4.3g
- Saturated Fat 0.7g
- Cholesterol 0mg
- Sodium 1715mg
- Total Carbs 74.8g
- Fiber 2.9g
- Sugars 3.3g
- Protein 13g

Creamy Garlic Chicken and Rice

Total Time: 50 minutes
Servings: 8

Ingredients:

- 1 teaspoon black pepper
- 6 garlic cloves, minced
- 5 cups chicken broth
- 4 tablespoons heavy cream
- 4 cups baby spinach
- 2 teaspoons garlic powder
- 2 tablespoons olive oil
- ½ cup long-grain white rice
- 2-pound chicken breasts, cut into chunks
- 1 teaspoon salt

Method:

1. Season the chicken breasts with garlic powder, salt, and black pepper.
2. Put olive oil in the Instant Zest Rice and Grain Cooker and add garlic and chicken breasts.
3. Press "Sauté" and adjust the timer to 15 minutes.
4. Open the lid and add rice, chicken broth, and spinach.
5. Secure the lid and press the "White Rice" button.
6. Add heavy cream and press "Steam."
7. Adjust the timer for about 10 minutes and dish out to serve.

Nutritional Value:

- Calories 347
- Total Fat 15.7g
- Saturated Fat 4.8g
- Cholesterol 111mg
- Sodium 881mg
- Total Carbs 12g
- Fiber 0.7g
- Sugars 0.7g
- Protein 37.5g

Chapter 4: Brown Rice Recipes

Simple Brown Rice

Total Time: 30 minutes
Servings: 4

Ingredients:

- 1 cup of brown rice
- 1¼ cups water

Method:

1. Put brown rice and water in the Instant Zest Rice and Grain Cooker.
2. Secure the lid and press the "Brown Rice" button.
3. Instant Zest Cooker will automatically shut down when the rice is completely cooked.
4. Fluff the rice and dish out to serve hot.

Nutritional Value:

- Calories 172
- Total Fat 1.3g
- Saturated Fat 0.3g
- Cholesterol 0mg
- Sodium 2mg
- Total Carbs 36.2g
- Fiber 1.6g
- Sugars 0g
- Protein 3.6g

Chicken Burrito Bowls

Total Time: 1 hour
Servings: 12

Ingredients:

- 4 teaspoons salt
- 30-ounce black beans, boiled
- 2 cups frozen corn kernels
- 2 teaspoons ground cumin
- 2 cups brown rice, uncooked
- 2 (14.5-ounce cans) diced tomatoes
- 4 teaspoons chili powder
- 3 pounds chicken breasts, boneless and skinless
- 2 cups low-sodium chicken broth

Method:

1. Mix together the chicken, diced tomatoes, chicken broth, chili powder, cumin, and salt in the Instant Zest Rice and Grain Cooker.
2. Secure the lid and press the "Steam" button.
3. Adjust the timer for about 20 minutes and open the lid after 20 minutes
4. Stir in the rice, beans, and corn and press "Brown Rice" button.
5. Instant Zest Cooker will automatically shut down when the rice is completely cooked.
6. Fluff the rice and dish out to serve hot.

Nutritional Value:

- Calories 615
- Total Fat 10.7g
- Saturated Fat 2.8g
- Cholesterol 101mg
- Sodium 1045mg
- Total Carbs 77.9g
- Fiber 14g
- Sugars 4.7g
- Protein 52.3g

Lentil and Brown Rice Tacos

Total Time: 35 minutes
Servings: 4

Ingredients:

- ¼ teaspoon onion powder
- ¼ teaspoon paprika
- ½ teaspoons salt
- 1/8 teaspoon red pepper flakes
- 1 teaspoon cumin
- ½ teaspoon black pepper
- ¼ cup of brown rice
- 3 garlic cloves, minced
- 1 tablespoon chili powder
- ½ cup green lentils
- ½ onion, diced
- 2 cups of water

Method:

1. Put brown rice and lentils with all other ingredients in the Instant Zest Rice and Grain Cooker.
2. Secure the lid and press the "Brown Rice" button.
3. Instant Zest Cooker will automatically shut down when the rice is completely cooked.
4. Fluff the rice and dish out to serve hot.

Nutritional Value:

- Calories 146
- Total Fat 1.1g
- Saturated Fat 0.2g
- Cholesterol 0mg
- Sodium 314mg
- Total Carbs 27.1g
- Fiber 8.9g
- Sugars 1.3g
- Protein 7.8g

Balsamic Brown Rice Bowl

Total Time: 35 minutes

Servings: 6

Ingredients:

- 4 cups of water
- 2 teaspoons red pepper flakes
- 4 cups baby spinach
- Balsamic glaze, for drizzling
- Extra-virgin olive oil, for drizzling
- Kosher salt and black pepper, to taste
- 2 lemons, halved
- 2 teaspoons Italian seasoning
- 2 cups fresh mozzarella, chopped
- Flaky sea salt
- 6 cups cherry tomatoes
- 2-pounds boneless skinless chicken breast
- 2 cups brown rice

Method:

1. Put brown rice with all other ingredients in the Instant Zest Rice and Grain Cooker.
2. Cover the lid and press the "Brown Rice" button.
3. Instant Zest Cooker will automatically shut down when the rice is completely cooked.
4. Fluff the rice and dish out in a bowl to serve hot.

Nutritional Value:

- Calories 612
- Total Fat 18g
- Saturated Fat 4.9g
- Cholesterol 141mg
- Sodium 215mg
- Total Carbs 58.6g
- Fiber 5.5g
- Sugars 5.5g
- Protein 53.6g

Black Beans with Brown Rice

Total Time: 35 minutes
Servings: 4

Ingredients:

- 4 oz pancetta, chopped
- 7 oz. black beans, rinsed
- Sea salt and black pepper, to taste
- ½ cup brown rice, rinsed
- ½ head of garlic, roasted
- 1 cup boiling water

Method:

1. Pour boiling water into the Instant Zest Rice and Grain Cooker and add brown rice, garlic, pancetta, and black beans.
2. Cover the lid and press the "Brown Rice" button.
3. Instant Zest Cooker will automatically shut down when the rice is completely cooked.
4. Fluff the rice and dish out to serve hot.

Nutritional Value:

- Calories 412
- Total Fat 13.2g
- Saturated Fat 4.2g
- Cholesterol 31mg
- Sodium 659mg
- Total Carbs 50.2g
- Fiber 8.4g   3
- Sugars 1.1g
- Protein 23.1g

Tomato, Brown Rice and Chickpea Stew

Total Time: 40 minutes

Servings: 2

Ingredients:

- 1 teaspoon Herbs de Provence
- ¼ cup of brown rice
- ½ can chickpeas, drained and rinsed
- ½ medium onion, thinly sliced
- 1 can diced tomatoes, low sodium
- 1 large cloves garlic, pressed
- 1 cup vegetable broth

Method:

1. Put brown rice with all other ingredients in the Instant Zest Rice and Grain Cooker.
2. Secure the lid and press the "Brown Rice" button.
3. Instant Zest Cooker will automatically shut down when the rice is completely cooked.
4. Fluff the rice and dish out in a bowl to serve hot.

Nutritional Value:

- Calories 324
- Total Fat 4.6g
- Saturated Fat 0.7g
- Cholesterol 0mg
- Sodium 436mg
- Total Carbs 56.9g
- Fiber 11.3g
- Sugars 9.3g
- Protein 15.2g

Spiced Lentils with Brown Rice and Chicken

Total Time: 55 minutes
Servings: 4

Ingredients:

- ½ tablespoon ginger, freshly grated
- ½ tablespoon ground cumin
- ½ teaspoon ground cardamom
- 1/8 teaspoon black pepper
- 1 garlic clove, minced
- ½ teaspoon ground cinnamon
- 1/8 teaspoon ground cloves
- Kosher salt, to taste
- ½ cup lentils
- 7-ounce diced tomatoes
- 1½ cups chicken broth
- ½-pound boneless skinless chicken breasts, cut into 1-inch pieces
- ½ cup of brown rice
- ½ red onion, diced
- 1 tablespoon olive oil
- ½ bay leaf

Method:

1. Put olive oil in the Instant Zest Rice and Grain Cooker and add onion, garlic, ginger, and bay leaf.
2. Press "Sauté" and sauté for about 3 minutes.
3. Add chicken, tomatoes, salt, and black pepper and sauté for about 5 minutes on each side.
4. Open the lid and add the rest of the ingredients.
5. Secure the lid and press the "Brown Rice" button.
6. Instant Zest Cooker will automatically shut down when the rice is completely cooked.
7. Fluff the rice and dish out in a bowl to serve hot.

Nutritional Value:

- Calories 347
- Total Fat 9.5g
- Saturated Fat 2g
- Cholesterol 50mg
- Sodium 381mg
- Total Carbs 38g
- Fiber 9.6g
- Sugars 2.7g
- Protein 27.1g

Brown Rice Pilaf

Total Time: 55 minutes
Servings: 3

Ingredients:

- 1 cup brown rice, rinsed and drained
- ¼ teaspoon salt
- 7-ounce chicken broth
- 2-ounce sliced mushrooms, drained
- ½ teaspoon dried thyme leaves
- ¼ cup onions, finely chopped
- Black pepper, to taste
- ¼ cup of water
- 1 tablespoon butter, softened

Method:

1. Mix together brown rice, onion, chicken broth, salt, water, black pepper, mushrooms, and thyme in the Instant Zest Rice and Grain Cooker.
2. Secure the lid and press the "Brown Rice" button.
3. Instant Zest Cooker will automatically shut down when the rice is completely cooked.
4. Fluff the rice and dish out in a bowl to serve hot.

Nutritional Value:

- Calories 282
- Total Fat 6g
- Saturated Fat 2.9g
- Cholesterol 10mg
- Sodium 436mg
- Total Carbs 50.1g
- Fiber 2.6g
- Sugars 0.9g
- Protein 6.9g

Chicken and Wild Brown Rice

Total Time: 55 minutes
Servings: 2

Ingredients:

- 1 cup yellow onions, thinly sliced
- ½ cup uncooked wild rice
- 4 oz button mushrooms, sliced
- 1 teaspoon salt
- ¼ teaspoon black pepper
- 2 tablespoons flat-leaf parsley, chopped
- 1 cup chicken broth
- ½ cup carrots, diced
- 1 tablespoon butter, melted
- 2 bone-in skin-on chicken thighs
- ½ tablespoon fresh thyme leaves, chopped

Method:

1. Mix together onions, broth, carrots, wild rice, mushrooms, and 1 teaspoon salt in the Instant Zest Rice and Grain Cooker.
2. Mix together the remaining 1 teaspoon salt, melted butter, chicken, and black pepper and transfer to the Zest Cooker.
3. Secure the lid and press the "Brown Rice" button.
4. Instant Zest Cooker will automatically shut down when the rice is completely cooked.
5. Fluff the rice and dish out in a bowl to serve hot.

Nutritional Value:

- Calories 499
- Total Fat 26g
- Saturated Fat 10.7g
- Cholesterol 113mg
- Sodium 1685mg
- Total Carbs 41.2g
- Fiber 5.4g
- Sugars 6.2g
- Protein 28g

Wild Brown Rice with Cranberries

Total Time: 55 minutes

Servings: 2

Ingredients:

- 1/8 teaspoon black pepper
- 1 can vegetable broth
- ¼ cup almonds, slivered
- 2 ounces sliced mushrooms, undrained
- ¼ cup dried cranberries
- ½ tablespoon butter, melted
- 2 tablespoons green onions, sliced
- ½ cup uncooked wild rice
- ¼ teaspoon salt

Method:

1. Combine all the ingredients in the Instant Zest Rice and Grain Cooker except almonds and cranberries.
2. Secure the lid and press the "Brown Rice" button.
3. Instant Zest Cooker will automatically shut down when the rice is completely cooked.
4. Cook almonds in a skillet for about 5 minutes over medium-low heat, stirring constantly.
5. Open the Instant Zest Cooker and top the rice with almonds and cranberries.
6. Press "Steam" and adjust the timer to 8 minutes.
7. Fluff the rice and dish out to serve hot.

Nutritional Value:

- Calories 300
- Total Fat 11g
- Saturated Fat 2.8g
- Cholesterol 8mg
- Sodium 1260mg
- Total Carbs 36.3g
- Fiber 4.9g
- Sugars 3.5g
- Protein 15.4g

Cumin and Parsley Brown Rice

Total Time: 45 minutes

Servings: 2

Ingredients:

- ½ cup of brown rice
- ¼ teaspoon butter
- 2 tablespoons parsley, chopped
- ½ cup of water
- 1 teaspoon cumin

Method:

1. Put butter in the Instant Zest Rice and Grain Cooker and add cumin.
2. Press "Sauté" and adjust the timer to 1 minute.
3. Open the lid and add rice, water, and parsley.
4. Secure the lid and press the "Brown Rice" button.
5. Instant Zest Cooker will automatically shut down when the rice is completely cooked.
6. Fluff the rice and dish out to serve hot.

Nutritional Value:

- Calories 181
- Total Fat 2g
- Saturated Fat 0.6g
- Cholesterol 1mg
- Sodium 11mg
- Total Carbs 36.9g
- Fiber 1.9g
- Sugars 0.1g
- Protein 3.9g

Chicken Tikka Masala Brown Rice

Total Time: 55 minutes
Servings: 3

Ingredients:

- 1 teaspoon coriander
- 1½ teaspoons salt
- 14-ounce diced tomatoes
- ½ cup fresh cilantro, diced
- 1 tablespoon salted butter
- 1 teaspoon paprika
- 2 tablespoons heavy cream
- 1 cup of brown rice
- 1½ cups water
- ½ onion, diced
- 1½ tablespoons ginger, freshly grated
- 1 tablespoon garam masala
- ½-pound chicken thighs, boneless, skinless
- 2½ garlic cloves, minced
- 1 tablespoon tomato paste

Method:

1. Put the chicken, butter, onion, garlic, ginger, tomatoes, tomato paste, garam masala, coriander, paprika, and salt in a wok.
2. Cover the lid and cook for about 8 minutes on medium-high heat.
3. Transfer it into the Instant Zest Rice and Grain Cooker and add rice and water.
4. Secure the lid and press the "Brown Rice" button.
5. Instant Zest Cooker will automatically shut down when the rice is completely cooked.
6. Stir in the heavy cream and cover the lid.
7. Press "Steam" and adjust the timer to 8 minutes.
8. Fluff the rice and dish out to serve hot.

Nutritional Value:

- Calories 494
- Total Fat 15.5g
- Saturated Fat 6.7g
- Cholesterol 91mg
- Sodium 4384mg
- Total Carbs 59.8g
- Fiber 5.2g
- Sugars 5.2g
- Protein 29.2g

Caramelized Ginger Chicken with Sticky Rice

Total Time: 55 minutes
Servings: 12

Ingredients:

- 1 cup light brown sugar
- ½ cup of vegetable oil
- 12 scallions, chopped
- 4 cups of water
- 3 tablespoons white vinegar
- 8 medium shallots
- 1 cup fresh ginger
- 1 cup pickled daikon
- 5 cups brown rice
- 2 cups + 4 tablespoons Asian fish sauce
- 8 whole chicken legs
- 6 tablespoons soy sauce
- 2 tablespoons honey
- 8 garlic cloves
- 6 Thai chilis
- Salt, to taste

Method:

1. Mix 4 tablespoons of the brown sugar with 4 tablespoons of the fish sauce in a dish.
2. Add chicken legs and coat them thoroughly with the marinade.
3. Let the chicken refrigerate overnight and transfer it in a wok.
4. Stir in the remaining ingredients except for rice and water and cook, covered for about 12 minutes.
5. Transfer it into the Instant Zest Rice and Grain Cooker and add rice and water.
6. Secure the lid and press the "Brown Rice" button.
7. Instant Zest Cooker will automatically shut down when the rice is completely cooked.

8. Dish out the rice in a bowl and serve hot.

Nutritional Value:

- Calories 696
- Total Fat 21.1g
- Saturated Fat 5g
- Cholesterol 63mg
- Sodium 4972mg
- Total Carbs 85.7g
- Fiber 4.3g
- Sugars 15.6g
- Protein 38g

Thai Sweet Brown Rice with Mango

Total Time: 50 minutes
Servings: 12

Ingredients:

- ½ cup of sugar
- 2 cups brown rice
- 8 mangoes
- 2 cups of coconut milk

Sauce

- 2 cans of coconut milk
- 2 tablespoons corn starch
- 6 tablespoons sugar
- ½ teaspoon salt
- 2 tablespoons sesame seeds, toasted lightly

Method:

1. Put the coconut milk, brown rice, and sugar in a wok.
2. Cover the lid and cook on low heat for about 1 hour.
3. Transfer into the Instant Zest Rice and Grain Cooker and add rice.
4. Secure the lid and press the "Brown Rice" button.
5. Instant Zest Cooker will automatically shut down when the rice is completely cooked.
6. Mix together coconut milk, corn starch, sugar, and salt in a bowl.
7. Drizzle the sauce on the top of rice and garnish with sesame seeds and mango to serve.

Nutritional Value:

- Calories 468
- Total Fat 21.5g
- Saturated Fat 17.4g
- Cholesterol 0mg
- Sodium 113mg
- Total Carbs 69.5g
- Fiber 6.6g
- Sugars 38.8g
- Protein 6.3g

Chicken Veggies and Rice

Total Time: 55 minutes
Servings: 12

Ingredients:

- 3 cups low sodium chicken broth
- 1 onion, finely diced
- 2 teaspoons Italian seasoning
- 1 teaspoon salt
- ½ teaspoon black pepper
- 2 cups frozen peas
- 1 cup milk
- 4 large carrots, peeled and finely diced
- 1 cup roasted red peppers, chopped
- 2 teaspoons garlic, minced
- 4 boneless skinless chicken breasts
- 4 cups brown rice
- 4 cups mozzarella cheese, shredded

Method:

1. Mix together broth, carrots, rice, onion, red peppers, Italian seasoning, peas, garlic, chicken breasts, salt, and black pepper in the Instant Zest Rice and Grain Cooker.
2. Secure the lid and press the "Brown Rice" button.
3. Instant Zest Cooker will automatically shut down when the rice is completely cooked.
4. Stir in the rest of the ingredients and cover the lid.
5. Press "Steam" and adjust the timer to 12 minutes.
6. Fluff the rice and dish out to serve hot.

Nutritional Value:

- Calories 404
- Total Fat 7.7g
- Saturated Fat 2.6g
- Cholesterol 51mg
- Sodium 395mg
- Total Carbs 58.1g
- Fiber 4.6g
- Sugars 4.5g
- Protein 24.5g

Garlic Butter Chicken and Rice

Total Time: 50 minutes
Servings: 12

Ingredients:

- 1 teaspoon garlic powder
- 8 tablespoons butter
- 8 large garlic cloves, minced
- 3 cups low-sodium, fat-free chicken broth
- 1 teaspoon dried Italian Seasoning
- Salt and black pepper, to taste
- Chopped fresh parsley, for garnish
- 2 teaspoons paprika
- 2 yellow onions, diced
- 3 cups brown rice
- 3 cups hot water
- 1 teaspoon dried oregano
- 12 skinless, bone-in chicken thighs
- 2 teaspoons dried thyme

Method:

1. Preheat oven to 350F.
2. Season chicken thighs with dried thyme, paprika, garlic powder, salt, and black pepper and keep aside.
3. Put butter in the Instant Zest Rice and Grain Cooker and add onions and garlic.
4. Press "Sauté" and adjust the timer to 3 minutes.
5. Add chicken and sauté for about 8 minutes.
6. Open the lid and add rice, chicken broth, Italian seasoning, oregano, and water.
7. Secure the lid and press the "Brown Rice" button.
8. Instant Zest Cooker will automatically shut down when the rice is completely cooked.
9. Garnish with fresh parsley and dish out to serve.

Nutritional Value:

- Calories 401
- Total Fat 13.2g
- Saturated Fat 6.7g
- Cholesterol 86mg
- Sodium 255mg
- Total Carbs 40.5g
- Fiber 2.4g
- Sugars 1g
- Protein 29.8g

Chapter 5: Lentils

Red Lentil Curry

Total Time: 40 minutes
Servings: 8

Ingredients:

- 6 tablespoons canola oil
- 4 tablespoons ginger, chopped
- 4 cloves garlic, chopped
- 16 scallions, sliced, white and green parts separated
- 2 tablespoons curry powder
- 8 carrots, chopped
- 2 russet potatoes, peeled and diced
- 2 cups red lentils
- 8 cups vegetable broth
- Salt and black pepper, to taste

Method:

1. Put oil in the Instant Zest Rice and Grain Cooker and add ginger, garlic, and scallion whites.
2. Press "Sauté" and adjust the timer to 3 minutes.
3. Open the lid and add the rest of the ingredients.
4. Secure the lid and press the "Mixed Grains" button.
5. Instant Zest Cooker will automatically shut down when the grains are completely cooked.
6. Dish out in a bowl and serve hot.

Nutritional Value:

- Calories 401
- Total Fat 11.6g
- Saturated Fat 1g
- Cholesterol 0mg
- Sodium 132mg
- Total Carbs 57.4g
- Fiber 19.5g
- Sugars 5.6g
- Protein 17.9g

Lentil Stew with Mustard Greens

Total Time: 50 minutes
Servings: 24

Ingredients:

- ½ tablespoon olive oil
- 3 cups chicken broth
- ½-pound Italian sausage links, casings removed
- 1 onion, chopped
- 1 garlic clove, chopped
- 3 cups kale and mustard greens, torn
- ½-pound sweet potatoes, peeled and diced
- ½ cup dried lentils
- Salt and black pepper, to taste

Method:

1. Put olive oil in the Instant Zest Rice and Grain Cooker and add garlic, onions, and sausages.
2. Press "Sauté" and adjust the timer to 12 minutes.
3. Open the lid and add broth, mustard greens, sweet potatoes, lentils, ½ teaspoon salt, and ¼ teaspoon pepper.
4. Secure the lid and press the "Mixed Grains" button.
5. Instant Zest Cooker will automatically shut down when the grains are completely cooked.
6. Dish out in a bowl and serve hot.

Nutritional Value:

- Calories 396
- Total Fat 17.7g
- Saturated Fat 5.7g
- Cholesterol 32mg
- Sodium 755mg
- Total Carbs 38.3g
- Fiber 11.7g
- Sugars 3.1g
- Protein 20.9g

Barley and Lentil Salad with Goat Cheese

Total Time: 50 minutes
Servings: 2

Ingredients:

- ½ cup barley
- 1½ tablespoons olive oil
- 1 tablespoon lemon juice
- Salt and black pepper, to taste
- ½ head romaine lettuce, torn
- 7-ounce lentils, rinsed
- ½ large carrot, julienned
- 1/8 small onion, chopped
- 2 tablespoons olives, pitted and chopped
- 1/8 English cucumber, diced
- 1-ounce goat cheese, crumbled

Method:

1. Put barley and water in the Instant Zest Rice and Grain Cooker.
2. Secure the lid and press the "Mixed Grains" button.
3. Instant Zest Cooker will automatically shut down when the grains are completely cooked.
4. Meanwhile, whisk together the oil, lemon juice, and ½ teaspoon each salt and pepper in a small bowl.
5. Toss the torn lettuce with one half of the lemon dressing in a medium bowl.
6. Mix together carrot, olives, lentils, onion, barley, and cucumber with the remaining lemon dressing in a second medium bowl.
7. Serve the barley mixture over the lettuce and sprinkle with the goat cheese.

Nutritional Value:

- Calories 633
- Total Fat 18.4g
- Saturated Fat 5.5g
- Cholesterol 15mg
- Sodium 152mg
- Total Carbs 86.6g
- Fiber 34.6g
- Sugars 5.4g
- Protein 33.7g

Lentil with Cabbage Slaw

Total Time: 40 minutes
Servings: 8

Ingredients:

- 30-ounce lentils, rinsed
- 1 cup fresh cilantro leaves
- 1 cup fresh flat-leaf parsley leaves
- 2 cloves garlic, chopped
- 4 tablespoons fresh lemon juice
- 1 cup panko crumbs
- Salt and black pepper, to taste
- ½ head red cabbage, shredded
- 6 tablespoons olive oil
- 1 teaspoon cumin ground
- 1 cup Greek yogurt
- ½ teaspoon red pepper, crushed
- 8 pitas, warmed

Method:

1. Put half of the lentils with the parsley, cilantro, garlic, and cumin in a food processor and process until smooth.
2. Transfer this blend to a bowl and mix in panko crumbs, the remaining lentils, ½ teaspoon salt, and ¼ teaspoon black pepper.
3. Form into ½-inch-thick patties.
4. Mash the cabbage lightly with the lemon juice, 1 tablespoon of the oil, and ¼ teaspoon each salt and black pepper in a large bowl and keep aside.
5. Mix together the yogurt, crushed red pepper, and ¼ cup water in a small bowl and keep aside.
6. Put remaining oil in the Instant Zest Rice and Grain Cooker and add patties.
7. Press "Sauté" and sauté for about 5 minutes on each side.
8. Top each pita with the patties, cabbage mixture, yogurt sauce, and the additional crushed red pepper and cilantro to serve.

Nutritional Value:

- Calories 722
- Total Fat 13.6g
- Saturated Fat 2.2g
- Cholesterol 2mg
- Sodium 449mg
- Total Carbs 114.2g
- Fiber 34.9g
- Sugars 10.1g
- Protein 36.3g

Winter Lentil Soup

Total Time: 45 minutes
Servings: 3

Ingredients:

- ½ tablespoon olive oil
- 2 leeks, sliced
- 14-ounce can tomatoes, drained
- 1 sweet potato, peeled and diced
- ½ bunch kale leaves, cut into strips
- ¼ cup brown lentils
- 3 cups of water
- ½ tablespoon fresh thyme, chopped
- Salt and black pepper, to taste
- 4 garlic cloves, chopped
- 2 tablespoons Parmesan, grated
- 3 Thai chilies
- Salt, to taste

Method:

1. Put oil in the Instant Zest Rice and Grain Cooker and add the leeks and tomatoes.
2. Press "Sauté" and adjust the timer to 8 minutes.
3. Stir in the sweet potatoes, kale, lentils, water, thyme, 1½ teaspoons salt, and ¼ teaspoon pepper.
4. Secure the lid and press the "Mixed Grains" button.
5. Instant Zest Cooker will automatically shut down when the grains are completely cooked.
6. Dish out in a bowl and top with the Parmesan to serve.

Nutritional Value:

- Calories 171
- Total Fat 3.9g
- Saturated Fat 1.1g
- Cholesterol 3mg
- Sodium 700mg
- Total Carbs 31.1g
- Fiber 4.6g
- Sugars 12.6g
- Protein 5.5g

Curried Lentils with Chicken and Potatoes

Total Time: 40 minutes
Servings: 12

Ingredients:

- 3 cups red lentils
- 3-pounds russet potatoes, peeled and diced
- 2 onions, chopped
- 4 garlic cloves, chopped
- 4 teaspoons curry powder
- 2 teaspoons fresh ginger chopped
- Salt and black pepper, to taste
- 8 cups chicken broth
- 12 chicken thighs, boneless and skinless
- 4 tablespoons lime juice
- ½ cup yogurt
- ½ cup fresh cilantro, chopped

Method:

1. Put the lentils, potatoes, onion, garlic, curry powder, ginger, 1¼ teaspoons salt, ¼ teaspoon pepper, broth, and chicken in the Instant Zest Rice and Grain Cooker.
2. Secure the lid and press the "Mixed Grains" button.
3. Instant Zest Cooker will automatically shut down when the grains are completely cooked.
4. Transfer the chicken to a medium bowl and shred it using 2 forks.
5. Stir in the lime juice and dish out to serve hot.

Nutritional Value:

- Calories 558
- Total Fat 11.7g
- Saturated Fat 3.2g
- Cholesterol 131mg
- Sodium 191mg
- Total Carbs 51.9g
- Fiber 18.1g
- Sugars 4.1g
- Protein 58.9g

Lentil Stew with Oranges

Total Time: 40 minutes
Servings: 2

Ingredients:

- 1 tablespoon olive oil
- 2 ounces Spanish chorizo sausage, thinly sliced
- ½ medium onion, peeled and finely chopped
- 1 clove garlic, peeled and finely chopped
- 1½ cups brown lentils washed and drained
- ½ cup dry red wine, such as Pinot Noir
- 1½ cups chicken broth
- 2 small oranges
- ½ teaspoon kosher salt
- ½ teaspoon freshly ground black pepper
- ½ cup chopped fresh dill

Method:

1. Put some oil in the Instant Zest Rice and Grain Cooker and add chorizo.
2. Press "Sauté" and adjust the timer to 5 minutes.
3. Dish out on a plate and keep aside.
4. Put the rest of the oil in the Instant Zest Rice and Grain Cooker and add garlic and onions.
5. Press "Sauté" and sauté for about 5 minutes.
6. Add the lentils and sauté for about 2 minutes.
7. Add the wine and broth and mix well.
8. Secure the lid and press the "Mixed Grains" button.
9. Instant Zest Cooker will automatically shut down when the grains are completely cooked.
10. Add chorizo, orange juice, dill, salt, and pepper and dish out in a bowl to serve hot.

Nutritional Value:

- Calories 383
- Total Fat 16.7g
- Saturated Fat 4.3g
- Cholesterol 0mg
- Sodium 1561mg
- Total Carbs 31.5g
- Fiber 7.9g
- Sugars 12.1g
- Protein 18.2g

Balsamic-Glazed Pork with Lentils

Total Time: 40 minutes
Servings: 2

Ingredients:

- ½ cup green lentils, rinsed
- Kosher salt and black pepper, to taste
- 1 tablespoon balsamic vinegar
- 1 tablespoon brown sugar
- 1½ tablespoons olive oil
- ½-pound pork tenderloin
- ½ red apple, cut into ½-inch pieces
- ½ celery stalk, thinly sliced
- 2 tablespoons fresh flat-leaf parsley leaves
- 4 cups of water
- 1 tablespoon fresh lemon juice

Method:

1. Preheat the oven to 400° F.
2. Put lentils and water in the Instant Zest Rice and Grain Cooker.
3. Secure the lid and press the "Mixed Grains" button.
4. Instant Zest Cooker will automatically shut down when the grains are completely cooked.
5. Meanwhile, combine the balsamic vinegar and brown sugar in a small bowl.
6. Put half of the oil over medium-high heat in a large ovenproof skillet and add pork, salt, and pepper.
7. Cook for about 6 minutes and transfer into the oven.
8. Roast for about 12 minutes, basting twice with the glaze.
9. Remove from the oven and cut into slices.
10. Mix together cooked lentils with the celery, apple, parsley, remaining oil, lemon juice, and ¼ teaspoon each salt and pepper.
11. Top with the pork and serve hot.

Nutritional Value:

- Calories 472
- Total Fat 15.2g
- Saturated Fat 3
- Cholesterol 83mg
- Sodium 89mg
- Total Carbs 41.4g
- Fiber 16.1g
- Sugars 11.4g
- Protein 42.3g

Salmon with Warm Lentil Salad

Total Time: 40 minutes

Servings: 2

Ingredients:

- ½ cup green lentils, rinsed
- Kosher salt and black pepper, to taste
- 1 tablespoon olive oil
- ½-pound skinless salmon fillet, cut into 4 pieces
- 1 tablespoon red wine vinegar
- 1 teaspoon Dijon mustard
- 1/8 red onion, chopped
- ¼ cup chopped fresh flat-leaf parsley
- 4 cups of water
- ½ bunch arugula, torn
- 1 lemon, cut into wedges

Method:

1. Put lentils, salt, and water in the Instant Zest Rice and Grain Cooker.
2. Secure the lid and press the "Mixed Grains" button.
3. Instant Zest Cooker will automatically shut down when the grains are completely cooked.
4. Dish out and drain the lentils.
5. Heat 1 teaspoon of the oil in the Instant Zest Rice and Grain Cooker and add salmon, salt, and pepper.
6. Press "Sauté" and sauté for about 5 minutes on each side.
7. Mix onion, vinegar, remaining 2 tablespoons of oil, mustard, salt, parsley, and pepper in a large bowl.
8. Stir in lentils and arugula to the vinegar mixture and toss to combine well.
9. Top with the salmon and lemon wedges to serve.

Nutritional Value:

- Calories 429
- Total Fat 15.8g

- Saturated Fat 3.1g
- Cholesterol 24mg
- Sodium 114mg
- Total Carbs 32.9
- Fiber 16g
- Sugars 2.2g
- Protein 40.5g

Red lentils with cauliflower and peanuts

Total Time: 40 minutes
Servings: 8

Ingredients:

- 2 white onions, peeled and diced
- 2 garlic cloves, minced
- 2 teaspoons fresh root ginger, finely diced
- 2 teaspoons mild curry powder
- 2 teaspoons fennel seeds
- 2 star anises
- 1 cinnamon stick
- 2 teaspoons garam masala
- 7 ounces unsalted butter
- 2 teaspoons olive oil
- 14 ounces red lentils, washed and soaked for 30 minutes
- 8 cups of water
- 7 ounces yogurt
- 7 ounces cream
- 2 cauliflowers, broken into florets, leaves reserved
- 2 lemons, juiced
- Salt, to taste
- 3 ounces peanuts
- 2 tablespoons fresh coriander, chopped

Method:

1. Put butter in the Instant Zest Rice and Grain Cooker and add onion, garlic, ginger, and spices.
2. Press "Sauté" and sauté for about 3 minutes.
3. Add the lentils, cream, half of the yogurt and water and stir well.
4. Secure the lid and press the "Mixed Grains" button.
5. Instant Zest Cooker will automatically shut down when the grains are completely cooked.

6. Deep fry the cauliflower until golden and squeeze with lemon juice, olive oil, and salt.
7. Dish out the lentils in a bowl and top with cauliflower leaves, peanuts, yogurt and coriander to serve.

Nutritional Value:

- Calories 544
- Total Fat 33.2g
- Saturated Fat 17.4g
- Cholesterol 74mg
- Sodium 247mg
- Total Carbs 45.2g
- Fiber 19.4g
- Sugars 8.4g
- Protein 20g

Halibut with Lentils and Mustard Sauce

Total Time: 40 minutes
Servings: 8

Ingredients:

- 4 tablespoons olive oil
- 2 large onions, chopped
- 4 cloves garlic, chopped
- 2 medium sweet potatoes, peeled and cut into 1/4-inch pieces
- 5 cups low-sodium chicken broth
- 3 cups green lentils, rinsed
- kosher salt and black pepper, to taste
- 8 halibut fillets
- ½ cup Dijon mustard
- ½ cup dry white wine
- 2 tablespoons fresh tarragon, chopped

Method:

1. Heat 1 tablespoon of the oil in the Instant Zest Rice and Grain Cooker and add onion, garlic, and sweet potato.
2. Press "Sauté" and sauté for about 6 minutes.
3. Add the broth, lentils, salt, and pepper and mix well.
4. Secure the lid and press the "Mixed Grains" button.
5. Instant Zest Cooker will automatically shut down when the grains are completely cooked.
6. Dish out the lentils in a bowl and keep aside.
7. Add the remaining oil, halibut, salt, and pepper in the Zest Cooker.
8. Press "Sauté" and sauté for about 5 minutes on each side.
9. Whisk together the mustard, wine, and tarragon in a bowl.
10. Divide the lentil mixture and halibut among plates and drizzle with the sauce to serve.

Nutritional Value:

- Calories 727
- Total Fat 15.2g
- Saturated Fat 2.1g
- Cholesterol 93mg
- Sodium 388mg
- Total Carbs 59.8g
- Fiber 24.9g
- Sugars 3.5g
- Protein 82.2g

Chapter 6: Beans

Big Beans and Tomato Vinaigrette

Total Time: 60 minutes
Servings: 8

Ingredients:

- 1 cup oregano sprigs
- 1 cup thyme sprigs
- 4 bay leaves
- 16 oz. dried butter beans, rinsed, soaked overnight and drained
- 4 cups of water
- 2 medium onions, halved
- 2 large carrots, scrubbed, coarsely chopped
- Kosher salt, to taste
- 1 cup extra-virgin olive oil
- 20 oz. cherry tomatoes or 1½ cups chopped heirloom or beefsteak tomatoes
- 2 garlic cloves, smashed
- ½ cup red wine vinegar
- 4 pounds assorted heirloom, beefsteak, and/or cherry tomatoes
- Freshly ground black pepper, to taste
- 1 cup basil leaves

Method:

1. Tie oregano, thyme, and bay leaves with kitchen twine.
2. Place these tied herbs in the Zest cooker, add beans, onions, carrots, and 4 cups water.
3. Secure the lid and press the "Mixed bean" button.
4. Instant Zest Cooker will automatically shut down when the beans are cooked.
5. Remove the lid and drain the beans then add them to a suitable bowl.
6. Blend cherry tomatoes in a blender until smooth, then add garlic, 1/3 cup oil, salt, and vinegar.
7. Mix it gently then leave for 20 minutes. Remove the garlic from the puree.

8. Add this puree to the beans, along with heirloom tomatoes and basil.
9. Toss well and serve
10. Serve.

Nutritional Value:

- Calories 405
- Total Fat 31.5g
- Saturated Fat 5.3g
- Cholesterol 7mg
- Sodium 133mg
- Total Carbs 26.4g
- Fiber 6g
- Sugars 4.8g
- Protein 7.9g

Green Bean Casserole

Total Time: 25 minutes
Servings: 12

Ingredients:

- 8 tablespoons unsalted butter, at room temperature
- 2 yellow onions, diced
- 16 ounces sliced button mushrooms
- Kosher salt and freshly ground black pepper, to taste
- 2 cups low-sodium chicken or vegetable broth
- 3 pounds green beans, trimmed and cut into bite-size pieces
- 2½ cups grated Parmesan
- 2 cups crispy fried onions
- 4 tablespoons all-purpose flour
- 1 cup heavy cream

Method:

1. Pour 1 cup water into the Zest cooker and place a steamer basket inside.
2. Spread all the green beans in the steamer basket.
3. Secure the lid and press the "Steam" button then increase the cooking time to 3 minutes.
4. Instant Zest Cooker will automatically shut down when the green beans are steamed.
5. Remove the lid and transfer the steamed beans to a suitable bowl.
6. Place a 2-quart saucepan over medium heat and add butter and onion.
7. Sauté for 4 minutes, then add mushroom, stir cook for 6 minutes.
8. Add salt, pepper, and broth then mix well.
9. Stir in flour, cream, parmesan, and dried onion until the sauce thickens.
10. Toss in the steamed beans and mix well.
11. Serve warm.

Nutritional Value:

- Calories 181
- Total Fat 11.9g

- Saturated Fat 7.3g
- Cholesterol 34mg
- Sodium 197mg
- Total Carbs 16.3g
- Fiber 5.4g
- Sugars 4.4g
- Protein 5.2g

Garlic Green Beans with Parmesan

Total Time: 35 minutes

Servings: 8

Ingredients:

- 4 tablespoons olive oil
- 4 tablespoons parsley, chopped
- 3/2 teaspoon black pepper
- 2 pounds green beans, washed
- 2 tablespoon garlic, chopped
- 2 teaspoons salt
- ½ cup parmesan cheese, grated

Method:

1. Pour 1 cup water into the Zest cooker and place a steamer basket inside.
2. Spread all the green beans in the steamer basket.
3. Secure the lid and press the "Steam" button then increase the cooking time to 6 minutes.
4. Instant Zest Cooker will automatically shut down when the beans are steamed.
5. Remove the lid and transfer the steamed green beans to a salad bowl.
6. Sauté garlic with oil in a pan for 30 seconds, then add salt and black pepper.
7. Add this mixture to the green beans and mix well to coat.
8. Drizzle parmesan cheese on top.
9. Serve.

Nutritional Value:

- Calories 122
- Total Fat 8.7g
- Saturated Fat 2g
- Cholesterol 5mg
- Sodium 655mg
- Total Carbs 9.3g
- Fiber 4g
- Sugars 1.6g
- Protein 4.5g

Party time Beans

Total Time: 50 minutes
Servings: 32

Ingredients:

- 3 cups ketchup
- 2 medium onions, chopped
- 2 medium green peppers, chopped
- 2 medium sweet red peppers, chopped
- 1 cup of water
- 1 cup packed brown sugar
- 4 bay leaves
- 6 teaspoons cider vinegar
- 2 teaspoons ground mustard
- ¼ teaspoon pepper
- 32 ounces kidney beans, rinsed and drained
- 30 ounces great northern beans, rinsed and drained
- 30 ounces lima beans
- 30 ounces black beans, rinsed and drained
- 30 ounces black-eyed peas, rinsed and drained

Method:

1. Add beans, peas and all other ingredients to the Zest cooker.
2. Secure the lid and press the "Mixed bean" button.
3. Instant Zest Cooker will automatically shut down when the beans are cooked.
4. Remove the lid and transfer the beans to a suitable bowl.
5. Discard the bay leaves.
6. Serve warm.

Nutritional Value:

- Calories 373
- Total Fat 1.6g
- Saturated Fat 0.3g
- Cholesterol 0mg
- Sodium 269mg
- Total Carbs 71.2g
- Fiber 16.4g   5
- Sugars 12.5g
- Protein 21.7g

Black-Eyed Peas with Ham

Total Time: 60 minutes
Servings: 8

Ingredients:

- 8 ounces black-eyed peas, dried
- 2 cups of water
- ½ cup ham, cooked and diced
- 1½ cloves garlic, minced
- ½ onion, chopped
- 1 teaspoon salt
- ½ teaspoon black pepper
- Green onions, sliced

Method:

1. Add black eyes peas, water, garlic, ham, onion, salt, and black pepper to the Zest cooker.
2. Secure the lid and press the "Mixed bean" button.
3. Instant Zest Cooker will automatically shut down when the beans are cooked.
4. Remove the lid and transfer the beans to a suitable bowl.
5. Drain the excess liquid from the black-eyed peas and garnish with green onions.
6. Serve warm.

Nutritional Value:

- Calories 62
- Total Fat 1.5g
- Saturated Fat 0.4g
- Cholesterol 8mg
- Sodium 493mg
- Total Carbs 8g
- Fiber 2g
- Sugars 0.5g
- Protein 4.7g

Vibrant Black-Eyed Pea Salad

Total Time: 50 minutes
Servings: 5

Ingredients:

- 16 ounces black-eyed peas, rinsed and drained
- 1 cup grape tomatoes, halved
- ½ each of the green, yellow and red peppers, finely chopped
- ½ small red onion, chopped
- ½ celery rib, chopped
- 4 cups of water
- 1 tablespoon minced fresh basil
- ½ cup red wine vinegar or balsamic vinegar
- ½ tablespoon mustard ground
- ½ teaspoon minced fresh oregano
- 3/2 teaspoon salt
- ¼ teaspoon black pepper
- 2 tablespoons olive oil

Method:

1. Add black-eyed peas and water to the Zest cooker.
2. Secure the lid and press the "Mixed bean" button.
3. Instant Zest Cooker will automatically shut down when the beans are cooked.
4. Remove the lid and drain the beans then transfer them to a salad bowl.
5. Toss in the celery, basil, peppers, onion, tomatoes, and peas.
6. Whisk salt, black pepper, oregano, mustard, and vinegar in a small bowl.
7. Pour this salad dressing into the beans then toss well.
8. Serve fresh.

Nutritional Value:

- Calories 135
- Total Fat 6.6g
- Saturated Fat 0.8g
- Cholesterol 0mg
- Sodium 510mg
- Total Carbs 15.1g
- Fiber 3.7g
- Sugars 1.9g
- Protein 5g

Perfect Pinto Beans

Total Time: 60 minutes
Servings: 6

Ingredients:

- ½ pound pinto beans
- 1 cup of water
- 1 teaspoon chili powder
- ½ teaspoon ground cumin
- ¼ teaspoon paprika
- 1/8 teaspoon cayenne
- 2 thick-cut slices of bacon, cut into thirds
- 1½ cloves garlic
- 1 bay leave
- ½ medium onion, diced
- ½ red bell pepper, diced
- Salt and black pepper

Method:

1. Add water, beans, and all other ingredients to the Zest cooker.
2. Secure the lid and press the "Mixed bean" button.
3. Instant Zest Cooker will automatically shut down when the beans are cooked.
4. Remove the lid and mix the cooked beans gently.
5. Serve warm.

Nutritional Value:

- Calories 176
- Total Fat 3.3g
- Saturated Fat 1g
- Cholesterol 7mg
- Sodium 156mg
- Total Carbs 26.1g
- Fiber 6.5g
- Sugars 1.7g
- Protein 10.8g

Green Beans and Bacon

Total Time: 20 minutes
Servings: 16

Ingredients:

- 5 pounds green beans, trimmed
- Salt, to taste
- 1-pound bacon, chopped
- 2 yellow onions, chopped
- 6 cloves garlic, minced
- 2 teaspoons red pepper flakes
- 1 cup pecans, chopped toasted
- Juice of 1 lemon
- Freshly ground pepper, to taste

Method:

1. Pour 1 cup water into the Zest cooker and place a steamer basket inside.
2. Spread all the green beans in the steamer basket.
3. Secure the lid and press the "Steam" button then increase the cooking time to 3 minutes.
4. Instant Zest Cooker will automatically shut down when the green beans are steamed.
5. Remove the lid and transfer the steamed beans to a salad bowl.
6. Place the 1-quart pan over medium heat and add bacon.
7. Sauté it until crispy then transfer to a plate.
8. Now add onion and garlic to the same pan and sauté for 5 minutes.
9. Transfer this onion mixture to the green beans along with sautéed bacon.
10. Add salt, black pepper, pecans, red pepper flakes, and lemon juice.
11. Toss the beans well and serve.

Nutritional Value:

- Calories 216
- Total Fat 13.3g
- Saturated Fat 4.1g
- Cholesterol 31mg
- Sodium 664mg
- Total Carbs 12.4g
- Fiber 5.4g
- Sugars 2.5g
- Protein 13.5g

Escarole with Cannellini Beans

Total Time: 70 minutes
Servings: 8

Ingredients:

- 2 sweet onions, halved
- 2 heads of garlic, halved
- 2 medium carrots, scrubbed
- 4 sprigs parsley
- 4 3-inch sprigs rosemary
- 4 sprigs sage
- 4 cups dried cannellini beans, soaked overnight, drained
- 8 cups of water
- 1 teaspoon freshly cracked black pepper

To assemble:

- 1½ cups olive oil, divided
- 4 garlic cloves, sliced
- 4 bay leaves
- 1 teaspoon crushed red pepper flakes
- 2 heads of escarole, leaves torn
- 2 ounces grated Parmesan
- Kosher salt, freshly ground pepper

Method:

1. Add beans, water, garlic, carrot, onion, parsley, pepper, sage, and rosemary to the Zest cooker.
2. Secure the lid and press the "Mixed bean" button.
3. Instant Zest Cooker will automatically shut down when the beans are cooked.
4. Remove the lid and drain the beans then transfer them to a suitable bowl.
5. Add 4 tbsp oil to a 2-quart pot and place it over medium heat.
6. Stir in garlic and sauté for 3 minutes, then add red pepper flakes, parsley, and bay leaves.

7. Stir cook for 30 seconds then add escarole leaves. Cook them for 5 minutes.
8. Pour in ½ cup water and let them cook for 25 minutes then add cooked beans.
9. Cook this mixture to a simmer.
10. Add Parmesan and adjust seasoning with salt and black pepper.
11. Serve warm.

Nutritional Value:

- Calories 724
- Total Fat 40.9g
- Saturated Fat 6.8g
- Cholesterol 5mg
- Sodium 132mg
- Total Carbs 70.6g
- Fiber 29.5g
- Sugars 4.5g
- Protein 27.2g

Marinated Beans with Celery and Ricotta Salata

Total Time: 50 minutes
Servings: 16

Ingredients:

- 30-oz. cannellini beans, rinsed
- 6 cups of water
- 8 celery stalks, thinly sliced
- ½ cup extra-virgin olive oil
- 1½ cups white wine vinegar
- 4 tablespoons chopped thyme
- Kosher salt, to taste
- 8 oz. ricotta Salata, crumbled
- Black pepper, to taste

Method:

1. Add beans and water to the Zest cooker.
2. Secure the lid and press the "Mixed bean" button.
3. Instant Zest Cooker will automatically shut down when the beans are cooked.
4. Remove the lid and transfer the beans to a salad bowl using a slotted spoon.
5. Stir in salt, vinegar, oil, celery, thyme, black pepper, and Ricotta Salata.
6. Toss them well and serve.

Nutritional Value:

- Calories 146
- Total Fat 10.8g
- Saturated Fat 3.2g
- Cholesterol 15mg
- Sodium 268mg
- Total Carbs 8.5g
- Fiber 2.3g
- Sugars 0.2g
- Protein 5g

Chapter 7: Steamed Vegetables

Steamed Potatoes

Total Time: 15 minutes
Servings: 8

Ingredients:

- 4 pounds Yukon Potatoes, sliced
- 4 tablespoons olive oil
- 2 teaspoons salt
- Black pepper, to taste
- Juice and zest of 2 lemons
- 4 tablespoons fresh herbs, chopped

Method:

1. Pour 1 cup water into the Zest cooker and place a steamer basket inside.
2. Spread all the potato slices in the steamer basket.
3. Secure the lid and press the "Steam" button then increase the cooking time to 8 minutes.
4. Instant Zest Cooker will automatically shut down when the potatoes are steamed.
5. Remove the lid and transfer the steam potatoes to a salad bowl.
6. Add olive oil, black pepper, salt, lemon juice, and lemon zest to season the potatoes.
7. Mix them well and serve.

Nutritional Value:

- Calories 129
- Total Fat 7.2g
- Saturated Fat 1g
- Cholesterol 0mg
- Sodium 591mg
- Total Carbs 16.6g
- Fiber 1.6g
- Sugars 0.9g
- Protein 1.9g

Steamed Pumpkin

Total Time: 20 minutes
Servings: 12

Ingredients:

- 7-ounce pumpkin, peeled and diced
- 2 tablespoons honey
- 4 teaspoons soy sauce

Method:

1. Pour 1 cup water into the Zest cooker and place a steamer basket inside.
2. Spread all the pumpkin cubes in the steamer basket.
3. Secure the lid and press the "Steam" button then increase the cooking time to 6 minutes.
4. Instant Zest Cooker will automatically shut down when the pumpkin is steamed.
5. Remove the lid and transfer the pumpkin to a salad bowl.
6. Pour honey and soy sauce on top, then toss well.
7. Serve.

Nutritional Value:

- Calories 34
- Total Fat 0.1g
- Saturated Fat 0.1g
- Cholesterol 0mg
- Sodium 201mg
- Total Carbs 8.7g
- Fiber 1g
- Sugars 6.9g
- Protein 0.6g

Steamed Vegetables with Chile-Lime Butter

Total Time: 20 minutes
Servings: 12

Ingredients:

- 4 tablespoons butter
- 2 cloves garlic, chopped
- 2 teaspoons lime peel, grated
- 2 teaspoons serrano, chopped
- 1 teaspoon salt
- 2 tablespoons fresh lime juice
- 6 cups fresh vegetables, such as cauliflower florets and broccoli florets

Method:

1. Pour 1 cup water into the Zest cooker and place a steamer basket inside.
2. Spread all the fresh vegetables in the steamer basket.
3. Secure the lid and press the "Steam" button then increase the cooking time to 6 minutes.
4. Meanwhile, place a 1-quart saucepan over low heat and butter to melt.
5. Stir in garlic and sauté for 20 seconds, then add salt, lime juice, chile, and lime peel.
6. Mix well and transfer this garlic mixture to a salad bowl
7. Instant Zest Cooker will automatically shut down when the vegetables are steamed.
8. Remove the lid and transfer the veggies to the salad bowl.
9. Toss the veggies with the garlic mixture for seasoning.
10. Serve.

Nutritional Value:

- Calories 56
- Total Fat 4.7g
- Saturated Fat 2.9g
- Cholesterol 12mg
- Sodium 320mg
- Total Carbs 3.4g
- Fiber 1.3g
- Sugars 0.8g
- Protein 0.7g

Steamed Vegetables with Sesame-Chile Oil

Total Time: 25 minutes
Servings: 8

Ingredients:

- 6 carrots, peeled and diced
- 2 tablespoons sesame-chili oil
- 16 spears asparagus, diced
- ½ head cauliflower, florets
- ½ head broccoli, florets
- 2 teaspoons olive oil
- 4 garlic cloves, chopped
- ½ teaspoon red pepper flakes
- Juice of 1 lemon
- Salt and black pepper, to taste

Method:

1. Pour 1 cup water into the Zest cooker and place a steamer basket inside.
2. Spread all the carrots, broccoli, cauliflower, and asparagus in the steamer basket.
3. Secure the lid and press the "Steam" button then increase the cooking time to 6 minutes.
4. Instant Zest Cooker will automatically shut down when the veggies are steamed.
5. Remove the lid and transfer the veggies to a salad bowl.
6. Place a 1-quart saucepan over medium heat and add sesame Chile oil, pepper flakes, garlic, and olive oil.
7. Stir cook this garlic mixture for 1 minute then transfer to the steamed veggies.
8. Toss them well then serve.

Nutritional Value:

- Calories 79
- Total Fat 4.7g
- Saturated Fat 0.7g
- Cholesterol 0mg
- Sodium 40mg
- Total Carbs 8.9g
- Fiber 3g
- Sugars 3.9g
- Protein 2.1g

Steamed Baby Vegetables

Total Time: 20 minutes
Servings: 4

Ingredients:

- 2 cups mini pattypan squash, trimmed
- 2 cups baby zucchini, trimmed
- 2 cups baby carrots, trimmed

Method:

1. Pour 1 cup water into the Zest cooker and place a steamer basket inside.
2. Spread squash, zucchini, and carrots in the steamer basket.
3. Secure the lid and press the "Steam" button then increase the cooking time to 8 minutes.
4. Instant Zest Cooker will automatically shut down when the veggies are steamed.
5. Remove the lid and transfer the steamed veggies to a salad bowl.
6. Serve fresh.

Nutritional Value:

- Calories 41
- Total Fat 0.2g
- Saturated Fat 0g
- Cholesterol 0mg
- Sodium 49mg
- Total Carbs 9.2g
- Fiber 2.6g
- Sugars 4.7g
- Protein 1.8g

Steamed Brussels Sprouts and Bacon

Total Time: 25 minutes

Servings: 8

Ingredients:

- 1 cup olive oil
- ½ tablespoon balsamic vinegar
- ½-pound bacon, 1-inch diced
- ½ cup chopped yellow onion
- ¼ cup shallots, sliced
- 6 ounces Brussels sprouts, trimmed and quartered
- Salt and black pepper, to taste
- ½ tablespoon butter, melted

Method:

1. Place a 1-quart saucepan over medium heat and add 1 tbsp olive oil
2. Stir in bacon and sauté for 7 minutes, then transfer it to a plate lined with paper towel.
3. Add shallots and onion to the same pan and stir cook for 5 minutes, then keep them aside.
4. Pour 1 cup water into the Zest cooker and place a steamer basket inside.
5. Spread all the Brussels sprouts in the steamer basket.
6. Secure the lid and press the "Steam" button then increase the cooking time to 5 minutes.
7. Instant Zest Cooker will automatically shut down when the Brussel sprouts are steamed.
8. Remove the lid and transfer the steamed Brussel sprouts to a salad bowl.
9. Toss in salt, black pepper, melted butter, balsamic vinegar, bacon, and sautéed onion mixture.
10. Mix well and serve.

Nutritional Value:

- Calories 318
- Total Fat 34.7g

- Saturated Fat 5.4g
- Cholesterol 3mg
- Sodium 15mg
- Total Carbs 4.6g
- Fiber 1.3g
- Sugars 1g
- Protein 1.3g

Steamed Vegetables with Herb Stir-Ins

Total Time: 20 minutes

Servings: 3

Ingredients:

- 1 tablespoon butter
- 1 tablespoon fresh herbs, chopped
- Salt and black pepper, to taste
- 2 cups mixed vegetables, diced

Method:

1. Pour 1 cup water into the Zest cooker and place a steamer basket inside.
2. Spread all the veggies in the steamer basket.
3. Secure the lid and press the "Steam" button then increase the cooking time to 6 minutes.
4. Instant Zest Cooker will automatically shut down when the veggies are steamed.
5. Remove the lid and transfer the steamed veggies to a salad bowl.
6. Add all the herbs, butter, salt, and black pepper.
7. Toss well and serve.

Nutritional Value:

- Calories 35
- Total Fat 3.9g
- Saturated Fat 2.4g
- Cholesterol 10mg
- Sodium 27mg
- Total Carbs 0.2g
- Fiber 0.2g
- Sugars 0g
- Protein 0.1g

Ginger Garlic Steamed Vegetables

Total Time: 30 minutes
Servings: 8

Ingredients:

- 2 heads cauliflowers, florets
- 4 cups sugar snap peas
- ½ cup olive oil
- 4 green onions, chopped in
- 2 red bell peppers, seeded and sliced
- 2 tablespoons rice vinegar
- 4 garlic cloves, minced
- 2 tablespoons fresh ginger, minced
- 1 teaspoon chili pepper flakes
- 1 teaspoon salt
- ½ teaspoon white pepper, ground
- ½ teaspoon Chinese five spice
- Fresh cilantro, to serve

Method:

1. Pour 1 cup water into the Zest cooker and place a steamer basket inside.
2. Spread cauliflower florets in the steamer basket.
3. Secure the lid and press the "Steam" button then increase the cooking time to 5 minutes.
4. Instant Zest Cooker will automatically shut down when the potatoes are steamed.
5. Remove the lid and add sugar snap peas, green onions, and bell peppers to the basket.
6. Secure the lid again and press the "Steam" button then increase the cooking time to minute.
7. Instant Zest Cooker will automatically shut down when the potatoes are steamed.
8. Remove the lid and transfer the steamed veggies to a salad bowl.
9. Meanwhile, mix the rest of the ingredients in a small bowl.
10. Pour this vinaigrette in the steamed vegetables.

11. Toss well and serve.

Nutritional Value:

- Calories 194
- Total Fat 13.1g
- Saturated Fat 1.9g
- Cholesterol 0mg
- Sodium 361mg
- Total Carbs 18g
- Fiber 7g
- Sugars 8.1g
- Protein 5.8g

Steamed Carrots with Butter

Total Time: 25 minutes

Servings: 12

Ingredients:

- 4 tablespoons butter
- 10 carrots, sliced
- 1 teaspoon salt
- Parsley or chives (chopped)

Method:

1. Pour 1 cup water into the Zest cooker and place a steamer basket inside.
2. Spread all the carrots in the steamer basket.
3. Secure the lid and press the "Steam" button then increase the cooking time to 6 minutes.
4. Instant Zest Cooker will automatically shut down when the potatoes are steamed.
5. Remove the lid and transfer the steamed carrots to a salad bowl.
6. Whisk butter with salt, parsley, or chives in a small bowl.
7. Pour this butter mixture over the steamed carrots and toss well.
8. Serve.

Nutritional Value:

- Calories 62
- Total Fat 3.8g
- Saturated Fat 2.4g
- Cholesterol 10mg
- Sodium 257mg
- Total Carbs 7g
- Fiber 1.3g
- Sugars 4.5g
- Protein 0.5g

Steamed Carrots

Total Time: 25 minutes
Servings: 2

Ingredients:

- 4 large carrots, sliced
- ½ teaspoon lemon juice
- ¼ teaspoon salt
- 1/8 teaspoon black pepper

Method:

1. Pour 1 cup water into the Zest cooker and place a steamer basket inside.
2. Spread all the carrots in the steamer basket.
3. Secure the lid and press the "Steam" button then increase the cooking time to 8 minutes.
4. Instant Zest Cooker will automatically shut down when the potatoes are steamed.
5. Remove the lid and transfer the steamed carrots to a salad bowl.
6. Whisk lemon juice, salt, and black pepper in a small bowl.
7. Pour this lemon juice mixture over the steamed carrots and toss well.
8. Serve.

Nutritional Value:

- Calories 60
- Total Fat 0g
- Saturated Fat 0g
- Cholesterol 0mg
- Sodium 390mg
- Total Carbs 14.3g
- Fiber 3.6g
- Sugars 7.1g
- Protein 1.2g

Steamed Carrots with Garlic-Ginger Butter

Total Time: 30 minutes

Servings: 8

Ingredients:

- 2 tablespoons butter
- 4 garlic cloves, minced
- 2 teaspoons fresh ginger, minced
- 2 tablespoons lime juice
- 2 tablespoons cilantro, chopped
- 2-pounds baby carrots, peeled
- 1 teaspoon lime rind, grated
- ½ teaspoon salt

Method:

1. Pour 1 cup water into the Zest cooker and place a steamer basket inside.
2. Spread all the carrots in the steamer basket.
3. Secure the lid and press the "Steam" button then increase the cooking time to 10 minutes.
4. Instant Zest Cooker will automatically shut down when the potatoes are steamed.
5. Remove the lid and transfer the steamed carrots to a salad bowl.
6. Place a 1-quart saucepan over medium heat and butter to melt.
7. Stir in garlic, and ginger then sauté for 1 minute.
8. Pour this butter garlic mixture over the steamed carrots and toss well.
9. Add cilantro, salt, lime juice, and lime rind then mix well.
10. Serve.

Nutritional Value:

- Calories 66
- Total Fat 2.9g
- Saturated Fat 1.8g
- Cholesterol 8mg
- Sodium 445mg
- Total Carbs 9.7g
- Fiber 3.1g
- Sugars 5g
- Protein 0.3g

Steamed Cauliflower with Herbs

Total Time: 20 minutes
Servings: 14

Ingredients:

- 2 head cauliflowers, cut into florets
- 8 teaspoons olive oil
- 3/2 teaspoon salt
- ½ teaspoon ground pepper
- 8 teaspoons fresh herbs, chopped

Method:

1. Pour 1 cup water into the Zest cooker and place a steamer basket inside.
2. Spread all the cauliflower florets in the steamer basket.
3. Secure the lid and press the "Steam" button then increase the cooking time to 6 minutes.
4. Instant Zest Cooker will automatically shut down when the potatoes are steamed.
5. Remove the lid and transfer the steamed cauliflower to a salad bowl.
6. Add herbs, olive oil, salt, and black pepper then toss well.
7. Serve.

Nutritional Value:

- Calories 34
- Total Fat 2.7g
- Saturated Fat 0.4g
- Cholesterol 0mg
- Sodium 12mg
- Total Carbs 2.3g
- Fiber 1.1g
- Sugars 0.9g
- Protein 0.8g

Conclusion

The Instant Zest Rice and Grain Cooker have changed the entire concept of cooking. The Smart Programs are a breakthrough in setting a perfect cooking time and temperature for your food. You can also use manual functions like sauté, risotto, steam, manual keep warm, and slow cook with adjustable temperature ranges. You can also prepare main dishes like veggies etc. with this amazing appliance. Moreover, time is money, and the preset Smart Programs in the device ensure that your food is ready for you in the shortest possible time with the minimum possible involved.

www.ingramcontent.com/pod-product-compliance
Lightning Source LLC
Chambersburg PA
CBHW081404070526
44583CB00020B/2669